EGYPT'S WILDLIFE
PAST AND PRESENT

DOMINIQUE NAVARRO

Scientific Consultants
Richard Hoath
Salima Ikram
John Wyatt
Matthew Lamanna

The American University in Cairo Press
Cairo • New York

The glorious remnants of Egypt's ancient civilization are some of the most awe-inspiring treasures we have on Earth. But the country also encompasses an exotic and mysterious abundance of wildlife, hiding in its temples and tombs, or persevering in its deserts, wadis, and oases.

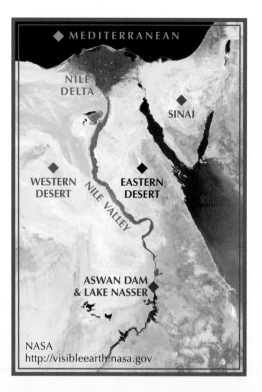

MEDITERRANEAN

NILE DELTA

SINAI

WESTERN DESERT

EASTERN DESERT

NILE VALLEY

ASWAN DAM & LAKE NASSER

NASA
http://visibleearth.nasa.gov

From space, Egypt is a vast expanse of arid desert covering over 90% of the country, with the Nile Valley a vein of green where humanity has thrived for thousands of years along the longest river in the world. Yet Egypt's diverse wildlife is to be found throughout the land—some rare and elusive, only to be encountered deep in the desert; others prolific and intrinsic to an Egyptian afternoon, like Barn Swallows at sunset. Egypt's species have evolved adaptations to cope with extreme temperatures and hostile rainless regions, from the Great Sand Sea of the Sahara to the mountainous terrain of the Eastern Desert and Sinai Peninsula. With each coastline and wetland, wadi (valley) and oasis, one discovers another community of animals and plants coexisting and surviving within their unique habitats.

◆ THE NILE DELTA & VALLEY

Following the river's banks as it winds south to north—from Aswan to Cairo into the Delta—the Nile Valley has been extensively cultivated and transformed by people, teeming with domesticated animals and introduced species of fruit and vegetable crops that grow year round. Yet a few natives can still be found, such as the Red Fox, Swamp Cat, Egyptian Weasel, Egyptian Mongoose, Lesser Egyptian Gerbil, and Cairo Spiny Mouse. The lush Valley habitat—with Date and Doum Palms—acts as a corridor for migrating birds that can be seen passing through seasonally to rest and feed among the populations of resident bird species like the Cattle Egret, Hoopoe, and Little Green Bee Eater. The wetland and desert habitats have an abundance of prey such as the Nile Valley Toad, African Chameleon, Saharan Fan-toed Gecko, Ocellated Skink, Scarlet Darter, Cairo Skipper, and Scarab Beetle.

Egypt's nocturnal canine species are rarely seen. The Jackal and foxes have been known to make their dens in natural caves as well as tombs.

Golden Jackal
Canis aureus

Wolf
Canis lupus

Red Fox
Vulpes vulpes

Rüppell's Sand Fox
Vulpes rueppellii

Blanford's Fox
Vulpes cana

Fennec Fox
Vulpes zerda

2

◆ SINAI

Sinai is a world unto itself, with snow on its mountain peaks, limestone plateaus, coastlines, and endemic flora and fauna in its wadis that can be found nowhere else in the world. Egypt's larger mammals find refuge here such as the Arabian Wolf, Blanford's Fox, and Sand Cat, while the Leopard is most likely now extinct. The smallest butterfly in the world—the Sinai Baton Blue—is found only here. Along the Mediterranean coastal desert of Sinai, the tiny and extremely rare Egyptian Tortoise is dependent on conservation efforts and protected areas such as Zaranik.

Sinai Baton Blue
Pseudophilotes sinaicus

◆ MEDITERRANEAN COASTAL ZONE

Vegetation and wildlife are more abundant in the north as one approaches the Mediterranean. With lower temperatures and higher precipitation, the narrow coast stretching from Alexandria to Libya supports a diverse range of wildlife habitats, home to the Cape Hare, Libyan Striped Weasel, and Long-eared Hedgehog. The Swamp Cat stalks birds in the reedbeds of the Nile Delta margins. Unfortunately, the climate and beauty of the Mediterranean Zone are also irresistible to tourists and the area is greatly threatened by overdevelopment.

◆ ASWAN DAM & LAKE NASSER

Egypt's environments were transformed with the completion of the Aswan High Dam in 1970, which provided stability to the country's water supply. The formation of Lake Nasser created new habitat and refuge for numerous birds as well as the Nile Crocodile, Nile Soft-shelled Turtle, and Nile Monitor, who rest along the shores among the last truly Nilotic vegetation of Acacia and Tamarisk. Freshwater fish thrive such as the Nile Perch and Vundu Catfish. In the remote regions around the lake, the Pharaoh Eagle Owl and Golden Jackal reside.

◆ RED SEA ISLANDS & MARINE HABITATS

The remarkable wildlife found throughout the mangroves and coral reefs of the Red Sea include Manta Rays, sharks, colorful fish and innumerable invertebrates. Over 40 uninhabited islands are valuable nesting habitats for both birds and sea turtles, while marine mammals include whales, dolphins, and Dugong. Several AUC Press publications explore the Red Sea's gorgeous and fragile environments.

◆ EASTERN DESERT WADIS & MOUNTAINS

Venturing between the Nile Valley and the Red Sea, the Qena–Safaga road winds through a rugged, mountainous terrain. Here the Egyptian Vulture soars overhead while sentries of Rock Hyrax stand guard. The moister wadi floor habitat nurtures Acacia trees and Tamarisk, Spiny Agama and Horned Viper, Bushy-tailed Jird and Dorcas Gazelle, Rüppell's Sand Fox and the elusive Caracal. Keeping to the mountains the last herds of Nubian Ibex and Barbary Sheep try to survive.

◆ WESTERN DESERT PLAINS & OASES

The vast arid plain of the Western Desert hides its marvels in a series of oases and unique features such as the Qattara Depression and White Desert. Here one might encounter the Fennec Fox, Striped Hyena, Lesser Egyptian Jerboa, and the Desert Monitor. This is home to the Dorcas Gazelle, the very rare Slender-horned Gazelle, and possibly the last of Egypt's Cheetahs. Herds of Addax and Slender-horned Oryx have sadly vanished. At the UNESCO World Heritage Site of the Valley of the Whales, or Wadi al-Hitan, prehistoric Basilosaurus whale fossils emerge from the ground. Between 250 and 35 million years ago, much of this desert was underwater with mangrove coastlines. Nearby in Bahariya Oasis, the fossils of some of the largest carnivorous dinosaurs have been found.

Egypt's elusive or rare feline species are adept hunters: the Cheetah can chase its prey at speeds of 100 kph; the Leopard ambushes; the Caracal will pounce on flocks of birds; the Swamp Cat's diet includes fish, while the desert-dwelling Sand Cat feeds on small rodents and reptiles such as geckos. The African Wild Cat is often confused with feral cats, a similar though smaller species.

Cheetah
Acinonyx jubatus

Caracal
Felis caracal

Leopard
Panthera pardus

Sand Cat
Felis margarita

Swamp Cat
Felis chaus

African Wild Cat
Felis silvestris lybica

EGYPT'S BIODIVERSITY TODAY:

MAMMALS	Nearly 100 including at least 13 marine species and over 20 bats
BIRDS	485 including over 170 resident and breeding species
INSECTS	Estimated 10,000–15,000
ARACHNIDS	Over 1,500 species including 24 scorpions
AMPHIBIANS	4 toads and 3 frogs
REPTILES	Approximately 100 including 24 geckos
FRESHWATER FISH	70–85 species
FRESHWATER INVERTEBRATES	Over 124 species
FLOWERING PLANTS	Over 2,000 including 62 endemics

Crested Lark
Galerida cristata

Yellow Wagtail
Motacilla flava

Eurasian Hoopoe
Upupa epops

Cairo Skipper
Spialia doris amenophis

Slender-horned Gazelle
Gazella leptoceros

Striped Hyena
Hyaena hyaena

House Sparrow
Passer domesticus

Scarlet Darter
Crocothemis erythraea

Tamarisk
Tamarix nilotica

Egyptian Locust
Anacridium aegyptium

Cape Hare
Lepus capensis

Swamp Cat
Felis chaus

Lesser Egyptian Jerboa
Jaculus jaculus

Horned Viper
Coluber cerastes

Cairo Spiny Mouse
Acomys cahirinus

Long-eared Desert Hedgehog
Hemiechinus auritus

Egyptian Tortoise
Testudo kleinmanni

Hooded Crow
Corvus cornix pallescens

Nile Acacia
Acacia nilotica

Black-winged Kite
Elanus caeruleus

Yellow-billed Kite
Milvus aegyptius

African Wild Ass
Equus africanus

Nubian Ibex
Capra nubiana

Egyptian Weasel
Mustela subpalmata

Egyptian Barbary Sheep
Ammotragus lervia ornatus

Dorcas Gazelle
Gazella dorcas

Ocellated Skink
Chalcides ocellatus

Egyptian Mongoose
Herpestes ichneumon

Rock Hyrax
Procavia capensis

Desert Monitor
Varanus griseus

Egyptian Cobra
Naja haje

Libyan Striped Weasel
Ictonyx libyca

Bushy-tailed Jird
Sekeetamys calurus

Camelthorn
Alhagi graecorum

Spiny Agama
Agama spinosa

Scarab Beetle
Scarabaeus sacer

Palestinian Yellow Scorpion
Leiurus quinquestriatus

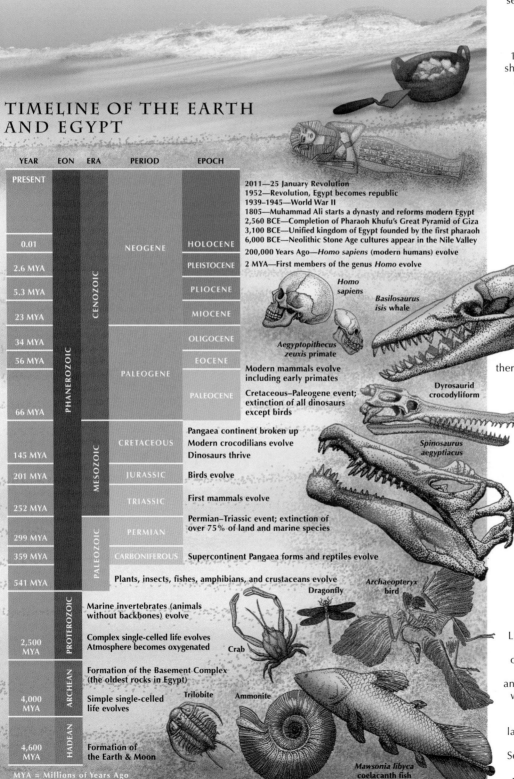

Egypt is very old. Dig down through the sand and rock layers and you will uncover a long and complex history going back over billions of years. Rocks record the events of Earth's past—from ice ages to the rise and fall of oceans to volcanic activity—and buried within them are the fossilized remains of plants and animals that evolved and died out millions of years ago...

TIMELINE OF THE EARTH AND EGYPT

YEAR	EON	ERA	PERIOD	EPOCH	
PRESENT					2011—25 January Revolution 1952—Revolution, Egypt becomes republic 1939–1945—World War II 1805—Muhammad Ali starts a dynasty and reforms modern Egypt 2,560 BCE—Completion of Pharaoh Khufu's Great Pyramid of Giza 3,100 BCE—Unified kingdom of Egypt founded by the first pharaoh 6,000 BCE—Neolithic Stone Age cultures appear in the Nile Valley
0.01	PHANEROZOIC	CENOZOIC	NEOGENE	HOLOCENE	200,000 Years Ago—Homo sapiens (modern humans) evolve
2.6 MYA				PLEISTOCENE	2 MYA—First members of the genus Homo evolve
5.3 MYA				PLIOCENE	
23 MYA				MIOCENE	
34 MYA			PALEOGENE	OLIGOCENE	
56 MYA				EOCENE	
66 MYA				PALEOCENE	Modern mammals evolve including early primates Cretaceous–Paleogene event; extinction of all dinosaurs except birds
145 MYA		MESOZOIC	CRETACEOUS		Pangaea continent broken up Modern crocodilians evolve Dinosaurs thrive
201 MYA			JURASSIC		Birds evolve
252 MYA			TRIASSIC		First mammals evolve
299 MYA		PALEOZOIC	PERMIAN		Permian–Triassic event; extinction of over 75% of land and marine species
359 MYA			CARBONIFEROUS		Supercontinent Pangaea forms and reptiles evolve
541 MYA					Plants, insects, fishes, amphibians, and crustaceans evolve
2,500 MYA	PROTEROZOIC				Marine invertebrates (animals without backbones) evolve Complex single-celled life evolves Atmosphere becomes oxygenated
4,000 MYA	ARCHEAN				Formation of the Basement Complex (the oldest rocks in Egypt) Simple single-celled life evolves
4,600 MYA	HADEAN				Formation of the Earth & Moon

MYA = Millions of Years Ago

Homo sapiens

Aegyptopithecus zeuxis primate

Basilosaurus isis whale

Dyrosaurid crocodyliform

Spinosaurus aegyptiacus

Archaeopteryx bird

Dragonfly

Crab

Trilobite

Ammonite

Mawsonia libyca coelacanth fish

CRETACEOUS DINOSAURS from 95 Million Years Ago
THEROPODS were bipedal (walking on two legs) and usually carnivorous. SAUROPODS were quadrupedal (walking on four legs) and herbivorous.

Spinosaurus aegyptiacus ①
"Egyptian spine lizard"
17 meters long—Possibly the longest of all theropods, with distinctive features including a narrow, crocodile-like skull, conical teeth, and a striking sail or hump-like protrusion supported by long spines arising from the backbone. Probably had a semiaquatic lifestyle and an opportunistic diet that included fish.

Carcharodontosaurus saharicus ②
"Saharan shark-toothed lizard"
14 meters long—Gigantic theropod with short arms, an enormous skull and jaws, and huge, serrated teeth—similar to those of a great white shark—which could be up to 20 centimeters in length.

Bahariasaurus ingens ③
"Enormous Bahariya lizard"
10 meters long—Large theropod known only from very incomplete fossils. Because so little material of Bahariasaurus has been discovered, many aspects of the appearance and lifestyle of this theropod remain mysterious. Deltadromeus, a theropod from similarly-aged rocks in Morocco, may actually be the same dinosaur as Bahariasaurus.

Aegyptosaurus baharijensis ④
"Egypt's lizard from Bahariya"
15 meters long—Medium-sized sauropod belonging to the subgroup Titanosauria, which were the most diverse and abundant sauropods in the southern continents during the Cretaceous Period. It was preyed upon by Carcharodontosaurus and probably Spinosaurus. Like those of Bahariasaurus, Ernst Stromer's fossils of this species—destroyed during World War II—are the only ones that have been discovered so far.

Paralititan stromeri ⑤
"Stromer's tidal giant"
26 meters long—Enormous titanosaur. Like all sauropods, Paralitian had a small skull, a long neck and tail, and four column-like limbs. It is one of the largest and heaviest dinosaurs ever discovered anywhere in the world. Fully-grown adults were probably immune to attack by even the largest predators. The only known skeleton was found in rocks that were laid down on a plant-covered tidal flat on the southern shore of the ancient Tethys Seaway. Among other kinds of vegetation, Paralititan fed upon the Cretaceous mangrove tree fern Weichselia reticulata.

When one thinks of Egypt, "the land of the pharaohs," an array of associations may come to mind: its ancient civilization and modern Arabic culture, its deserts and camels... But few people realize Egypt is also home to some of the greatest paleontological discoveries in the world.

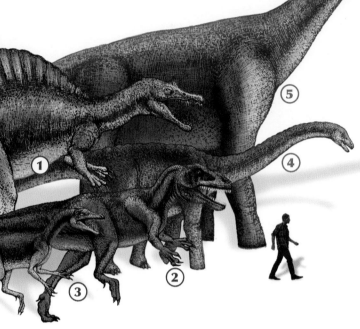

EGYPT'S DINOSAURS

Dinosaurs ruled the Earth from about 230 to 66 million years ago. But it wasn't until 1911 that a German paleontologist, Ernst Freiherr Stromer von Reichenbach, traveled via steamship, train, and camel to explore Egypt's Western Desert near Bahariya Oasis where he discovered the roughly 95 million-year-old fossils of Cretaceous dinosaurs: the huge theropods *Spinosaurus aegyptiacus*, *Carcharodontosaurus saharicus*, and *Bahariasaurus ingens*; the long-necked, plant-eating sauropod *Aegyptosaurus baharijensis*; and *Stomatosuchus inermis*, a huge and strange crocodyliform (a relative of modern crocodiles).

Egypt's prehistoric secrets have only begun to be revealed. Foreign occupations, wars, revolutions, and the harsh Saharan environment have made it notoriously difficult for scientists to explore the region. In 2000, an Egyptian and American team excavated in Bahariya and became the first researchers in over 80 years to find dinosaur skeletons in the oasis. Among a number of exciting discoveries were the fossils of a new sauropod, *Paralititan stromeri*, one of the largest land animals known to science. Many of the fossils the team collected, including *Paralititan*, are on display at the Egyptian Geological Museum in Cairo.

Dr. Matthew Lamanna and a humerus bone of ***Paralititan stromeri*** found by the Bahariya Dinosaur Project team in Egypt, 2000. Photo courtesy Dr. Josh Smith

VALLEY OF THE WHALES

Egypt possesses seven breathtaking UNESCO World Heritage Sites, including the Great Pyramids of Giza, the Theban Necropolis near Luxor, and one of immense paleontological importance: Wadi al-Hitan, the Valley of the Whales.

The Fayoum Oasis in the Western Desert—less than two hours' drive from Cairo—is an intriguing and beautiful place: birds and fish thrive in Birket (Lake) Qarun, locals enjoy the waterfalls of Wadi al-Rayan Protectorate, and further into the desert, the fossilized remains of ancient whales lie exposed in the sand at Wadi al-Hitan. It is extraordinary to imagine that this arid region was once submerged under the Tethys Seaway.

Among the many Eocene fossils at Wadi al-Hitan are the remains of some of the earliest and most primitive whales. Two species are most frequently found here: the lengthy *Basilosaurus isis* and a similar but smaller whale called *Dorudon atrox*. Remarkable for many reasons, these ancient mammals are significant for their hind limbs: small, probably functionless "legs," complete with feet and toes, that provide indisputable evidence that whales evolved from land-living mammals.

EGYPT ◆

EARLY EOCENE 56 Million Years Ago

TETHYS SEAWAY

The Tethys Seaway submerged large regions of Europe, Asia, and North Africa, including Egypt, during the early Eocene.

Dorudon atrox "Fierce spear tooth" 5 meters long

Functionless hind limb.

Basilosaurus isis "King lizard of Isis" 18 meters long— Possibly the largest Eocene mammal.

Barn Owl
Tyto alba

Kuhl's Pipistrelle
Pipistrellus kuhlii

Lesser Kestrel
Falco naumanni

Brown-necked Raven
Corvus ruficollis

Barn Swallow
Hirundo rustica

Acacia
Acacia nilotica

Leopard
Panthera pardus

Dorcas Gazelle
Gazella dorcas

Scimitar Oryx
Oryx dammah

Addax
Addax nasomaculatus

Little Egret
Egretta garzetta

Glossy Ibis
Plegadis falcinellus

Yellow Pansy Butterfly
Junonia hierta cebrene

Fennec Fox
Vulpes zerda

Nile Crocodile
Crocodylus niloticus

White Water Lily
Nymphaea lotus

Griffon Vulture
Gyps fulvus

Egyptian Vulture
Neophron percnopterus

Date Palm
Phoenix dactylifera

Doum Palm
Hyphaene thebaica

Egyptian Goose
Alopochen aegyptiacus

Barbary Falcon
Falco pelegrinoides

Giraffe
Giraffa camelopardalis

Sycomore Fig
Ficus sycomorus

Papyrus
Cyperus papyrus

Spotted Hyena
Crocuta crocuta

Sand Cat
Felis margarita

Northern Lapwing
Vanellus vanellus

Hippopotamus
Hippopotamus amphibius

Hamadryas Baboon
Papio hamadryas

Levant Green Frog
Pelophylax bedriagae

Wandering through the towering pillars of Karnak Temple, or into the depths of tombs in the Valley of the Kings, admirers of ancient Egypt will suddenly find themselves on safari surrounded by wildlife. Carved reverently into the walls, a menagerie of exotic creatures abound: hieroglyphs, paintings, and sculpted reliefs depict lions and jackals, falcons and ibises, cobras and scarabs. Animals played many vital roles in ancient Egyptian civilization—as sustenance, beasts of burden, or devoted companions—and they were an eternal source of inspiration for language, artwork, and religious beliefs.

Predynastic rock drawing near Silwa Bahari.

EGYPT'S PREDYNASTIC ENVIRONMENT

Egypt was not always the hot, arid desert it is known for today. Ten thousand years ago—long before the first pharaoh—it is believed Egypt was a thriving territory of grassy veldt, rich with a diverse array of wildlife, lush vegetation, and reliable rainfall. The land was ruled by a variety of mighty animals including Lions, African Elephants, and Black Rhinoceros. The River Nile was wild and untamed, reigned over by massive Hippopotamuses and impressive Nile Crocodiles. Majestic herds of Giraffe roamed the savanna alongside Addax, Bubal Hartebeest, Nile Lechwe, Scimitar Oryx, and Ostrich, stealthily stalked by African Wild Dogs, Cheetahs, Striped Hyenas, and early ancient Egyptians. Rock drawings dating from c. 6,000–4,000 BC depict such scenes.

By 3,000 BC, various factors including climatic changes, loss of habitat, and human expansion caused many animal species to start moving southward into sub-Saharan Africa, gradually becoming locally extinct. Ancient Egyptian civilization developed and prospered, despite the region growing arid and more hostile, suffering occasional severe droughts. Eventually, animals such as elephants, giraffe, and monkeys could only be found south of Egypt, and tomb scenes depict these "exotic" creatures being brought back as tribute for pharaoh. Thus, the artwork of the ancients is a glimpse of a changing world.

THE FIRST NATURALISTS

Ancient Egyptians were avid observers of nature. They were hunters, fowlers, and fishermen, and one of the earliest civilizations to master agriculture and domesticate animals. Survival in a wild world required a keen understanding of it. The ancients documented their environment in intricately illustrated scenes with details so precise that one can identify specific species among a flock of birds or a school of fish. Unique traits that identify an animal were also depicted, such as the lethally gaping mouth of a Hippopotamus, the hooded display of an Egyptian Cobra, or the regal crown feathers of a Hoopoe.

Horus at Edfu Temple. The sun god was a combination of Lanner, Barbary, and other falcons, making Horus a "super-raptor."

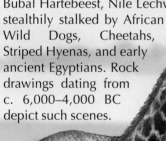

Bubal Hartebeest
Alcelaphus buselaphus

Nile Lechwe
Kobus megaceros

Black Rhinoceros
Diceros bicornis

African Elephant
Loxodonta africana

Giraffe
Giraffa camelopardalis

Ostrich
Struthio camelus

Striped Hyena
Hyaena hyaena

African Wild Dog
Lycaon pictus

Cheetah
Acinonyx jubatus

Lion
Panthera leo

WILD INCARNATIONS

Certain animal attributes became associated with divine qualities: the strength and virility of a bull was likened to that of the pharaoh; falcons soaring through the sky were affiliated to the god of the sun; and the crocodile was the feared lord of the Nile. Ancient Egyptians believed that animals had a direct relationship with the gods, speaking their secret language, and with powers such as creation and rebirth. Thus, animal cults grew within the civilization until nearly every village and town in ancient Egypt possessed its own animal god.

ANIMAL CULTS

Hathor

Ancient animal cults focused on a specific animal in which the spirit of a god resided, to be worshipped, and act as an oracle for the people. The bull cults were the most common, beginning as early as the First Dynasty (3050—2813 BC) in Memphis with the Apis Bull, embodying the creator god Ptah. Cows were also deified as the maternal protectress Hathor. Other cults included the ram god Khnum, the cat goddess Bastet, and the crocodile god Sobek.

Lotus • Nile Carp • Tadpole • Glossy Ibis • Crocodile • Barn Owl • Horned Viper • Quail Chick • Ram • African Hoopoe *Upupa epops* • Bee/Wasp • Pintail Duck • Cape Hare • Scarab • Giraffe • Lizard • Bull • Swallow • Papyrus • Lapwing • Egyptian Vulture • Canine

HIEROGLYPHIC FAUNA

The ancient Egyptians called their language of hieroglyphic symbols *medu netjeru*, "the gods' words." It is believed to be one of the oldest writing systems in the world and was in use for nearly four thousand years. Permeated with animal and plant imagery, it drew inspiration from nature and communicated religious beliefs, ideas, spells, and histories.

A hieroglyph could be a pictogram, illustrating an object, animal, or god; or the symbol may act as a phonogram to indicate a sound, much like modern alphabets: an Egyptian Vulture suggests the sound "a," the Barn Owl the sound "m," a Horned Viper the sound "f," while the image of a cat is pronounced "miw."

Hieroglyphs often conceal more complex messages, sometimes alluding to a character trait of an object or animal: a Giraffe means "to foretell" due to its ability to see further, while a tadpole indicates "millions," and a lizard represents "many." A combination of symbols might convey a more complex message: a Lapwing (a symbol called the *rekhyt*) with a basket beneath it and upraised arms translates into "all the people give praise." The Lappet-faced Vulture (goddess Nekhbet) came to represent the deity of Upper Egypt in the South, while the Egyptian Cobra (goddess Wadjet) was the deity of Lower Egypt; depicted together, resting on two baskets, they signify *nebty*, the "two ladies," representing unified Egypt.

Sekhmet, lioness warrior goddess

Khnum, ram-headed god and creator of other deities and human beings

Thoth, with the head of an ibis, was god of knowledge and writing

Thoth was also depicted as a baboon

Khepri, scarab god of creation and rebirth

Horus, raptor god of the sun

Sobek, crocodile god

Hamadryas Baboon *Papio hamadryas*

THE ETERNAL LIFE OF AN ANIMAL MUMMY

Mummification ensured that the body of a creature would be preserved forever, bestowing upon it eternal life. Ancient Egyptians mummified animals for several different purposes...

Osiris fish prepared by Anubis, god of mummification. Anubis is shown as a 'super-canid' combining the features of the nocturnal jackals, foxes, and dogs that haunted the necropolis cemeteries, and thus became associated with death.

Vervet Monkey
Chlorocebus pygerythrus

SACRED ANIMALS

A worshiped beast would be cared for throughout its lifetime by temple priests of an animal cult. Kept in a special sanctuary, it was indulged and adored as a god. Upon its death, the animal would be tenderly mummified and an elaborate funeral held with extensive mourning by the people. The mummy would then be placed in a coffin or sarcophagus and taken to a special cemetery with final rites administered. Soon thereafter, priests would locate a similar "marked" animal into which the spirit of the god would pass, and the cult ritual would continue.

Baby crocodile mummy.
Photo by Anna-Marie Kellen

VOTIVE OFFERINGS

Some animal mummies were prepared simply as gifts to the gods, offered by pilgrims visiting a cult shrine. At Saqqara's Sacred Animal Necropolis, where several animal deities were worshipped, 10,000 bird mummies were buried annually by pilgrims offering a prayer to the gods. The catacombs of Tuna al-Gebel—sacred to the god Thoth—are filled with ibis and baboon mummies, while burial grounds at Abydos contain the mummified remains of falcons and dogs. Other votive offerings included Nile Tilapia fish, Egyptian Cobras, Scarab Beetles, shrews, scorpions, and the eggs of birds and reptiles.

BELOVED PETS

Much like people today, ancient Egyptians adored their pets, and wanted to guarantee that such companions would remain at their side for all eternity in the Afterlife. From the Old Kingdom (2649—2150 BC) onward, depictions of beloved pets were carved or painted on tomb walls, such as the imagery of a cat or imported Vervet Monkey seated beneath the chair of its owner, or hunting scenes of a man accompanied by his dog or Egyptian Mongoose. Such artwork—as well as mummification of the animal upon its death—ensured the union of owner and pet in the Afterlife. A mummified pet might even be entombed beside its owner: Lady Isetemkheb was buried with her pet gazelle, while Hapymin of Abydos was buried with his pet dog curled up at his feet. Other pets included horses, donkeys, baboons, and birds. Pets might receive their own special coffin or sarcophagus, and funerary stela.

NOURISHMENT FOR THE AFTERLIFE

Ancient Egyptians led a rich life of bountiful hunting, fishing and farming. Tomb walls depict their feasts, and carefully wrapped "victual mummies" of meat and fowl were placed in burial chambers so that the deceased could dine on them in the Afterlife. Cattle, ducks, geese, pigeon, sheep, and goats were thoroughly prepared, salted in natron, dried, and wrapped in linen like traditional mummies. Tutankhamun was entombed with over forty cases of food mummies to sustain him for eternity.

The Cairo Museum holds the largest collection of animal mummies. Learn more about the **Animal Mummy Project:**
www.salimaikram.com

Griffon Vulture *Gyps fulvus*

ANCIENT AVIFAUNA

Wander into nearly any temple or tomb whose walls are graced with paintings and hieroglyphs and you will find yourself a keen bird watcher. The ancient Egyptians depicted over 100 different bird species in their art and as symbols in their writing. And in the open courtyards of antiquities such as Luxor Temple and Medinet Habu, look up and you will often find resident House Sparrows nesting or a Brown-necked Raven gazing down from atop the lofty temple walls.

Birds in ancient Egypt played a key role in everyday life. Some species were hunted while others were tenderly mummified like the pharaohs. Others inspired hieroglyphic symbols or were deified and venerated in wall paintings and sculpted reliefs.

While some species like the Ostrich, Lappet-faced Vulture, or Sacred Ibis are reverently depicted in ancient art, such birds have sadly become rare or locally extinct in Egypt due to overhunting and loss of habitat. Pollution has transformed the Nile waters, where Papyrus and Lotus swamps have long disappeared, forcing some migrants to adapt or seek sanctuary elsewhere. Some birds—like the Common Kestrel, Senegal Thick-knee, Common Bubul, and Pallid Swift—have adapted to modern, urban life in cities like Cairo.

Egyptian Fruit Bat *Rousettus aegyptiacus*

Oleander Sphinx Moth *Daphnis nerii*

Egyptian Nightjar *Caprimulgus aegyptius*

Pharaoh Eagle Owl *Bubo ascalaphus*

Barn Owl *Tyto alba*

Little Owl *Athene noctua*

The **Sacred Ibis**, *Threskiornis aethiopicus*, and an ibis coffin which contained the mummified remains of the bird. Millions of ibis mummies have been found at the animal necropolis of Saqqara.

NOCTURNAL ENCOUNTERS

With rising temperatures comes the summer drought or *Shemu* as it was known to the ancients. People, animals, and birds become creatures of the night. As the sun sets, a few charming residents, including Painted Snipe and Black-crowned Night Heron, may appear along the water's edge. The Egyptian Nightjar spends its days lying invisibly on desert sands but takes to the air at dusk with a moth-like flight. In the night sky, one would be very lucky to see the magnificent "eared" Pharaoh Eagle Owl, as it prefers desert regions, but some have been sighted nesting in the vicinity of the Giza and Saqqara Pyramids. The whiter Barn Owl can be easily distinguished passing silently overhead while a fleeting flash in the air above may not be a bird at all but rather the only mammal capable of bird-like flight: the bat. There are over 20 bat species in Egypt, the largest being the Egyptian Fruit Bat.

ASIA

EGYPT

AFRICA

Foreigners flock to Egypt, both tourists and birds alike. Egypt is a unique land bridge creating one of the world's largest bird migration systems, a route referred to as the **African-Eurasian Flyway**.

Of the 485 species of birds found in Egypt, over 170 are residents.

Eurasian Crane
Grus grus

White Stork
Ciconia ciconia

Great White Pelican
Pelecanus onocrotalus

Common Bulbul
Pycnonotus barbatus

Senegal Coucal
Centropus senegalensis

Masked Shrike
Lanius nubicus

Nile Valley Sunbird
Anthreptes metallicus

Giant Milkweed
Calotropis procera

Eurasian Hoopoe
Upupa epops

Grasshopper
Poekilocerus bufonius

Laughing Dove
Streptopelia senegalensis

In fall and again in spring, one can witness the passage of over five million birds all along the Nile on their journeys between Europe and Asia to central and southern Africa. The Nile is the life source for all of Egypt and creates a wealth of wetlands that are dense and diverse with bird species, an abundance of prey, and lush vegetation. As the seasons change and one travels from the Delta to the southernmost regions of the country, different bird species appear. These migrants feed and rest among the numerous resident species that call the Nile Valley home.

Osprey
Pandion haliaetus

Nile Carp
Labeo niloticus

Painted Lady
Vanessa cardui

Little Green Bee-eater
Merops orientalis

Egyptian Plover
Pluvianus aegyptius

Kentish Plover
Charadrius alexandrinus

Philae Temple

Nile Tilapia
Oreochromis niloticus

Great White Egret
Egretta alba

Common Moorhen
Gallinula chloropus

Purple Heron
Ardea purpurea

Little Egret
Egretta garzetta

Egyptian Goose
Alopochen aegyptiacus

Senegal Thick-knee
Burhinus senegalensis

Painted Snipe
Rostratula benghalensis

Purple Gallinule
Porphyrio porphyrio

Little Bittern
Ixobrychus minutus

Squacco Heron
Ardeola ralloides

Pallid Swift
Apus pallidus

White-breasted Kingfisher
Halcyon smyrnensis

Great Cormorant
Phalacrocorax carbo

Grey Heron
Ardea cinerea

Common Reed
Phragmites australis

Graceful Prinia
Prinia gracilis

Zitting Cisticola
Cisticola juncidis

Black-crowned Night Heron
Nycticorax nycticorax

Clamorous Reed Warbler
Acrocephalus stentoreus

NILE RIVER SPECIES

Throughout the Nile Valley are numerous and vital wetlands where a variety of freshwater fish and a gorgeous assortment of waterbirds thrive. A winter arrival to brackish lagoons, mainly in the north, is the Greater Flamingo. Flocks of hundreds settle into wetland areas such as Lake Qarun in the Fayoum region, a Natural Protectorate. A pinky-white species, the Flamingo has a distinctive, massive beak for just one purpose: filter feeding. With the aid of a large tongue and hair-like lamellae, water and soft mud are pressed and strained to leave a rich, edible mixture of algae, mollusks, and crustaceans. The Eurasian Spoonbill uses its spatula-shaped beak to sweep shallow waters for tiny fish and crustaceans. The Black-winged Stilt has a longish, needle-fine, straight beak, which, coupled with its extraordinarily long legs, enables it to wade and feed in deeper water. Although found in the same habitats, none of these species compete for food as their differently shaped bills necessitate differing feeding behaviors.

THE LEGACY OF CROCODILES

Egypt is home to the Nile Crocodile, *Crocodylus niloticus*, which was revered by ancient Egyptians as the river god Sobek and is a living reminder of Egypt's prehistoric legacy. Early crocodilians first appeared about 85 million years ago, near the end of the Cretaceous Period. Their supreme ability to adapt may have helped them to survive extreme adversity, including mass extinctions. Today, however, crocodilians are endangered, as they struggle to survive and compete with the greatest adversary they have encountered in their history: humans.

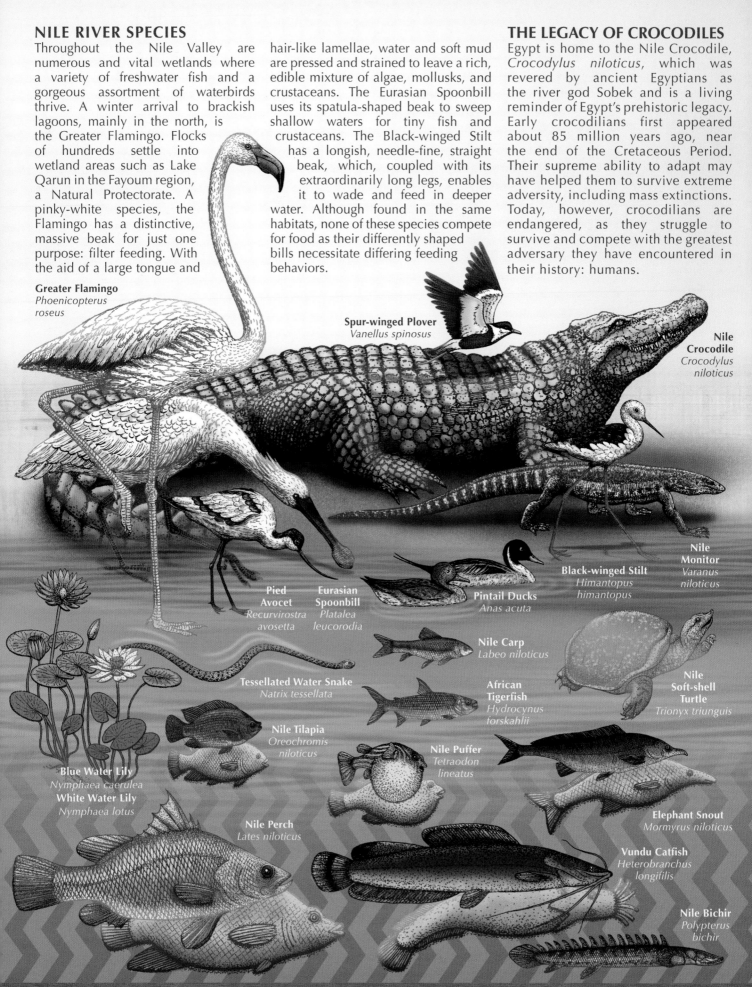

Greater Flamingo
Phoenicopterus roseus

Spur-winged Plover
Vanellus spinosus

Nile Crocodile
Crocodylus niloticus

Nile Monitor
Varanus niloticus

Pied Avocet
Recurvirostra avosetta

Eurasian Spoonbill
Platalea leucorodia

Pintail Ducks
Anas acuta

Black-winged Stilt
Himantopus himantopus

Nile Carp
Labeo niloticus

Nile Soft-shell Turtle
Trionyx triunguis

Tessellated Water Snake
Natrix tessellata

African Tigerfish
Hydrocynus forskahlii

Nile Tilapia
Oreochromis niloticus

Nile Puffer
Tetraodon lineatus

Blue Water Lily
Nymphaea caerulea
White Water Lily
Nymphaea lotus

Nile Perch
Lates niloticus

Elephant Snout
Mormyrus niloticus

Vundu Catfish
Heterobranchus longifilis

Nile Bichir
Polypterus bichir